# NEW AUNT JOURNAL

Record your special auntie experiences using words and pictures to create a family keepsake to treasure forever.

Aunt Name

_____

Baby Name

_____

Date of Birth

_____

Date:_____

_____

_____

_____

Date:_____

_____

_____

_____

Date:_____

_____

_____

_____

Date:_____

_____

_____

_____

Date:_____

_____

_____

_____

Date:_____

_____

_____

_____

Date:_____

_____

_____

_____

Date:_____

_____

_____

_____

Date:_____

_____

_____

_____

Date:_____

_____

_____

_____

Date:_____

_____

_____

_____

Date:_____

_____

_____

_____

Date:_____

_____

_____

_____

Date:_____

_____
_____
_____

Date:_____

_____
_____
_____

Date:_____

_____

_____

_____

Date:_____

_____

_____

_____

Date:_____

_____

_____

_____

Date:_____

_____

_____

_____

Date:_____

_____

_____

_____

Date:_____

_____

_____

_____

Date:_____

_____

_____

_____

Date:_____

_____

_____

_____

Date:_____

_____

_____

_____

Date:_____

_____

_____

_____

Date:_____

_____

_____

_____

Date:_____

_____

_____

_____

Date:_____

_____

_____

_____

Date:_____

_____

_____

_____

Date:_____

_____
_____
_____

Date:_____

Date:_____

_____

_____

_____

Date:_____

Date:_____

_____

_____

_____

Date:_____

_____
_____
_____

Date:_____

Date:_____

_____

_____

_____

Date:_____

_____
_____
_____

Date:_____

_____

_____

_____

Date:_____

_____

_____

_____

Date:_____

_____

_____

_____

Date:_____

_____

_____

_____

Date:_____

_____

_____

_____

Date:_____

_____

_____

_____

Date:_____

_____

_____

_____

Date:_____

_____
_____
_____

Date:_____

_____
_____
_____

Date:_____

_____

_____

_____

Date:_____

_____
_____
_____

Date:_____

_____

_____

_____

Date:_____

_____

_____

_____

Date:_____

_____
_____
_____

Date:_____

_____

_____

_____

Date:_____

_____

_____

_____

Date:_____

Date:_____

_____

_____

_____

Date:_____

_____
_____
_____

Date:_____

_____

_____

_____

Date:_____

_____

_____

_____

Date:_____

_____

_____

_____

Date:_____

_____

_____

_____

Date:_____

_____

_____

_____

Date:_____

_____

_____

_____

Date:_____

_____
_____
_____

Date:_____

_____
_____
_____

Date:_____

_____
_____
_____

Date:_____

_____
_____
_____

Date:_____

_____

_____

_____

Date:_____

_____

_____

_____

Date:_____

_____

_____

_____

Date:_____

_____
_____
_____

Date:_____

Date:_____

Date:_____

_____

_____

_____

Date:_____

_____

_____

_____

Date:_____

_____
_____
_____

Date:_____

_____

_____

_____

Date:_____

Date:_____

_____

_____

_____

Date:_____

_____

_____

_____

Date:_____

_____

_____

_____

Date:_____

_____

_____

_____

Date:_____

_____

_____

_____

Date:_____

_____

_____

_____

Date:_____

_____

_____

_____

Date:_____

_____
_____
_____

Date:_____

_____

_____

_____

Date:_____

Date:_____

Date:_____

_____
_____
_____

Date:_____

Date:_____

_____

_____

_____

Date:_____

_____

_____

_____

Date:_____

_____

_____

_____

Date:_____

_____

_____

_____

Date:_____

_____

_____

_____

Date:_____

_____

_____

_____

Date:_____

_____

_____

_____

Date:_____

_____

_____

_____

Date:_____

_____

_____

_____

Date:_____

_____

_____

_____

Date:_____

Date:_____

_____

_____

_____

Date:_____

_____
_____
_____

Date:_____

_____

_____

_____

Date:_____

_____
_____
_____

Date:_____

Date:_____

Date:_____

_____

_____

_____

Date:_____

_____

_____

_____

Date:_____

_____
_____
_____

Date:_____

_____

_____

_____

Date:_____

_____

_____

_____

Date:_____

_____

_____

_____

Date:_____

Date:_____

_____

_____

_____

Date:_____

Date:_____

_____

_____

_____

Made in the USA
Las Vegas, NV
05 November 2022

58824014R00072